A GIFT FROM THOSE WHO BUILT

THE COMMUNITY WALL

San Francisco Earthquake, 1989

Titles in the *American Disasters* series:

The Exxon Valdez
Tragic Oil Spill
ISBN 0-7660-1058-9

Hurricane Andrew
Nature's Rage
ISBN 0-7660-1057-0

The Oklahoma City Bombing
Terror in the Heartland
ISBN 0-7660-1061-9

Plains Outbreak Tornadoes
Killer Twisters
ISBN 0-7660-1059-7

San Francisco Earthquake, 1989
Death and Destruction
ISBN 0-7660-1060-0

The World Trade Center Bombing
Terror in the Towers
ISBN 0-7660-1056-2

San Francisco Earthquake, 1989

Death and Destruction

Victoria Sherrow

Enslow Publishers, Inc.

40 Industrial Road   PO Box 38
Box 398   Aldershot
Berkeley Heights, NJ 07922   Hants GU12 6BP
USA   UK

http://www.enslow.com

Library of Congress Cataloging-in-Publication Data

Sherrow, Victoria.
    San Francisco earthquake, 1989: death and destruction / Victoria
Sherrow.
        p. cm. —(American disasters)
    Includes bibliographical references and index.
    Summary: Details the events surrounding the earthquake that took
place in the San Francisco Bay Area in October 1989, as well as the
cleanup and recovery efforts that followed.
   ISBN 0-7660-1060-0
    1. Earthquakes—California—Loma Prieta—Juvenile literature.
2. Earthquakes—California—San Francisco Bay Area—Juvenile
literature. 3. Disaster relief—California—Loma Prieta—Juvenile
literature. 4. Disaster relief—California—San Francisco Bay Area—
Juvenile literature. [1. Earthquakes—California—San Francisco
Bay Area.] I. Title II. Series.
HV600.1989C2573   1998
363.34'95'0979461—dc21   97-39181
                                        CIP
                                        AC

Printed in the United States of America

10 9 8 7 6 5 4 3 2

Photo Credits: A/P Wide World Photos, pp. 1, 6, 8, 10, 11, 15, 17, 19, 20, 21,
23, 24, 25, 28, 30, 32, 34, 36, 38, 39, 41.

Cover Photo: A/P Wide World Photos

Contents

CHAPTER 1

Fifteen Seconds of Destruction

Baseball fans in northern California were especially excited about the 1989 World Series. Two local teams faced each other—the San Francisco Giants and the Oakland Athletics. Oakland fans were thrilled that their team had won the first two games. Giants fans hoped their team would come on strong and take the lead.

By late afternoon on October 17, some fifty-eight thousand fans had gathered at Candlestick Park for Game 3. About 50 million other fans were watching the players warm up on television. There were only sixteen more minutes until game time, as the clock struck 5:04 P.M. Pacific time.

Suddenly, the stands began to tremble. Television viewers stared at their sets in confusion. The baseball field seemed to be shaking. What was wrong with their televisions? People watching ABC television heard sportscaster Al Michaels say, "We're having an earth . . . !"[1] Then the screen went blank.

Back at Candlestick Park, people felt the earth tremble. Don Robinson, a pitcher for the Athletics, was just leaving the clubhouse. He later said, "I ran into the manager's office and dropped down on the floor."[2] Other players ran toward the stands to make sure that their wives and children were all safe.

The stunned crowd realized that an earthquake had struck. Police arrived and told people to move toward the exits. There would be no game tonight.

Fortunately, the stadium itself had held up and nobody was injured. Outside the park, spectators saw the damage that had occurred.

*O*nly minor repairs were needed at Candlestick Park following the earthquake that postponed Game 3 of the World Series.

Seventy-nine-year-old Alice Legare was at home when the quake struck. She was sitting on the sofa in her apartment near the San Francisco Bay. Her light fixtures and furniture began to jiggle. Legare realized it was an earthquake, and she tried to get outside. But the vibrations were too strong. Legare recalled:

> Every time I rose from the couch, the shaking pulled me down again. The building leaped, and everything in my room came crashing down. I held my ears and began yelling, "Oh, no! Oh, no!" I was sure the building would collapse.[3]

Thirteen-year-old Serina Johnson was at home with her eleven-year-old sister, Corina. Suddenly, food, dishes, and furniture began to fly around their apartment. They ran outside before the building began to collapse. Corina Johnson said, "It was like being in a blender."[4]

Some families had the added terror of being apart from each other during the quake. Gretchen Wells recalled: "I was at work in downtown San Francisco. My husband was here in the condominium. The baby was down the street. Luckily he was outside with his babysitter."[5]

Wells's husband, Don Dianda, recalls feelings of panic. He said,

> I was in the house at the time of the earthquake, and after being shaken around violently in here for fifteen seconds or so, I bolted for the front door and tried desperately to get it open, which is—I was unable to do—because I wanted so much to find my son. I was able to get through the back, and then out through the garage, and the first thing I saw were buildings laying in the street.[6]

*S*ome family members were in different places when the earthquake struck. Gretchen Wells was working in San Francisco, isolated from her husband and baby.

Dianda was relieved to find his son alive and well in the nearby park.

The quake had hit at a very bad time—rush hour. Tens of thousands of people were driving along local highways at this time of day. The San Francisco–Oakland Bay Bridge was seriously damaged. A fifty-foot-long piece of the road-way split off. It fell onto the lower deck, carrying cars along with it. One driver whose car plunged downward was killed.

A crane is positioned, ready to lift a section of the San Francisco–Oakland Bay Bridge that collapsed during the Bay Area earthquake.

A one-mile-long section of the Nimitz Freeway, part of Interstate Highway 880, collapsed. Petra Berumen had been driving along the Nimitz with a friend and Berumen's two children at 5:04 P.M. When the highway collapsed, Berumen's car was smashed, and she and her friend both died. Berumen's eight-year-old daughter, Cathy, suffered broken bones and other injuries. Six-year-old Julio Berumen was even worse off. He was trapped in the wreckage.

Julio and other survivors waited fearfully in a tangle of metal and concrete. As rescuers reached the scene, they could hear Julio and others crying out for help.

In the meantime people all over America heard about the disaster. Many reached for their telephones. They tried to check on friends and relatives who lived in the stricken area. There were about 20 million attempted phone calls that night.

Because so many people tried to call their family and friends at the same time, lines were overloaded. The telephone company responded to the emergency. They allowed only emergency phone calls to be put through during the next two days.

Later, scientists would rank this earthquake as the second worst in United States history. The San Francisco Bay Area earthquake, as the 1989 quake was called, caused dozens of deaths and hundreds of injuries. There were billions of dollars in losses. Once again, California had felt nature's fury.

CHAPTER 2

Rumblings of Disaster

This earthquake was not the first disaster of this kind to hit northern California. In fact, the worst earthquake in United States history also took place in San Francisco, in 1906. On that April day, hundreds of buildings shuddered and crumbled to the ground. Afterward, fires raged throughout the city. Water mains broke, and fire hoses lacked enough pressure to put out the flames. The fires caused even more damage than the quake itself. Seven hundred people died.

Like other earthquakes, the 1906 disaster caught people by surprise. Scientists cannot yet name the day or exact time that an earthquake will strike—as they can with hurricanes, for example. They can, however, predict *where* a quake will probably hit. In 1988 there was a 30 percent chance of a moderate-to-large earthquake in the San Francisco area. It struck in 1989.

Part of California lies above the San Andreas Fault. A fault is a place where rocks beneath the earth's surface have cracked and pulled away from their normal positions. Earthquakes occur when layers of the earth above a fault move along the cracked area.

The San Andreas Fault developed in two large pieces of rock. They are called the Pacific and North American plates. This fault is hundreds of miles long. It is called a strike-slip fault. This type of fault runs up and down. In strike-slip faults, one piece of rock moves past the rock on the opposite side. There are also two other types of faults. In a normal fault, one side of two opposite pieces of rock has been pulled downward. In reverse faults, the two sides of rock are shoved together. One side moves upward, so that it is higher than the other one.

The layers of rock in the earth's crust do not remain still. Forces within the earth cause rock to bend, twist, and turn. When plates move or bump or scrape each other, pressure builds up. This pressure stretches the rock. It is flexible enough to bend and stretch up to a point. When the strain becomes too strong, the rock cracks.

This release of energy causes the earth to move. When the rock moves along a fault, people above ground feel this jolt as an earthquake. When a rock along a crack moves slightly, people may not notice anything. Other times, the rock moves so much that it causes tremendous damage.

The two plates in the San Andreas Fault had been pushing at each other since the 1906 quake. In October 1989 scientists found that the Pacific Plate had moved about two kilometers (1.2 miles) northwest of the North

American Plate. It also moved upward about one kilometer (0.62 miles).[1]

When an earthquake occurs, scientists assign it a number on the Richter scale. The San Francisco Bay Area earthquake was rated a 7.0. The Richter scale tells the strength of a quake. Charles F. Richter developed the scale in 1935. It measures the energy released at the heart of the quake.

To reach this number, scientists look at the recordings on a seismograph. A seismograph is a device that shows earthquake waves. During the fifteen seconds of the San

A fourth-grade class in Oakland talks about the Bay Area earthquake. The force of the earthquake damaged their school and disrupted classes.

Francisco quake, seismic waves (waves of energy) spread from the original site of the quake.

The Richter scale begins with the number 1 and moves up. The higher the number, the stronger the quake. Each higher number means the quake was ten times stronger than the one below. For instance, a magnitude 5 on the Richter scale is ten times stronger than a magnitude 4.

The scale has no top number, but scientists think the limit is probably about 9.5. As of 1997, the strongest quake ever measured with the revised version of the Richter scale was around 9.2. This rating was given to a 1964 quake in Anchorage, Alaska. Quakes that register 8 or more have taken place only once every five to ten years.

There is a National Earthquake Information Center in Golden, Colorado. Scientists there gather information after a quake. They identified the epicenter of the San Francisco Bay Area quake. The epicenter is the area where damage is likely to be most severe.

The center also sends out questionnaires after an earthquake occurs. Police, firefighters, Red Cross workers, and others are asked to describe what happened. Scientists use this information to write reports and make maps. These maps show what kind of damage took place in different areas touched by the quake.

As scientists analyzed the earthquake, people in the stricken area felt numerous aftershocks. These are tremors that occur after a quake. The earth shakes as the rocks continues to settle into new positions. Sometimes, there are a few aftershocks. Other times, people endure dozens, or even hundreds of them. Aftershocks are frightening and can also cause additional problems due to broken gas pipes, fires, and further harm to damaged buildings.

Within a week of the quake, there were thousands of aftershocks. Some were as strong as 4.5 on the Richter scale. People faced an emergency situation and a long recovery process.

*B*uildings smolder after fires broke out. Fires are often started when aftershocks damage gas lines and knock buildings off their foundations.

CHAPTER 3

Miracle Survivors

David Gasser will never forget October 17, 1989. He was driving his truck south of San Francisco along Route 1. Suddenly, a huge landslide erupted right across the road. Gasser said it looked as if "the cliffs began exploding."[1] He grabbed his camera and began taking pictures.

In neighborhoods, streams of people could be seen leaving shattered buildings. They carried suitcases stuffed with clothing, other necessities, and treasured belongings. Some were able to move in with friends or relatives or pay for rooms in hotels. Many others went to emergency shelters. The Red Cross rushed to set up shelters.

Meanwhile, rescue crews raced to the Nimitz Freeway. Auto mechanic Richard Reynolds had seen Interstate Highway 880 crash onto the lower level. He said, "It just slid. It didn't fall. It just slid. You couldn't see nothing [sic] but dust. Then people came out of the dust."[2] Smoke rose from these smashed cars as many of them burst into flames. People were trapped in their cars and trucks in twisted mazes of metal and concrete. Twenty-two people died in the wreckage of the freeway.

Julio Berumen was trapped there for six hours. A team of doctors and firemen struggled in vain to pull him out. Dr. James Betts was one of those who risked their lives by crawling through the narrow space to reach the trapped six-year-old boy. Rescue workers and the doctors had to make a difficult decision. In order to free Julio and save his life, they had to amputate the boy's crushed left leg. News reporters told Julio's story, and he became known as the "miracle survivor."[3]

*R*esidents of the Marina District in San Francisco were given fifteen minutes to retrieve belongings from their damaged homes, following the earthquake.

After his rescue Julio Berumen was rushed to a hospital. He would later undergo several operations on his leg. For weeks Julio would be treated in a rehabilitation hospital. His eight-year-old sister, Cathy, also received medical care for her injuries. The children then had to deal with the tragic loss of their mother.

Tim Peterson, a twenty-five-year-old firefighter, was driving his pickup truck along I-880 when the highway collapsed. After the crash he was trapped inside his mangled truck. Peterson suffered terrible pain caused by numerous fractures and crushed bones in his legs. As time passed he lost hope. He felt sure he was going to die. However, Oakland firefighters managed to get him out about four hours after the quake. Peterson spent months in physical therapy, working hard to regain the use of his legs. In the end he was able to return to his fire-fighting unit.

The collapse of the Cypress Freeway in Oakland was also devastating. Forty-two other people died there. Dramatic rescues were taking place all over the city. In the

Six-year-old Julio Berumen had to have his leg amputated in order to free him from the collapsed Interstate 880 freeway, following the earthquake.

Marina District, fifty-six-year-old Sherra Cox was buried under the rubble of her apartment building. Firefighter Gerry Shannon worked for more than two hours to free her. Cox's home and all her possessions were lost in the quake. She suffered from a broken pelvis and a cracked hip.

Not everyone was lucky enough to survive. One fifty-seven-year-old longshoreman, Buck Helm, was rescued from highway wreckage four days after the quake. He was alive but critically injured. Helm died a month later as a result of his injuries.

*T*he body of one of the victims of the earthquake is removed from the rubble of a collapsed section of Highway I-880.

The Marina area was especially hard hit. One reason for this dates back to 1915. During that year San Francisco hosted an international fair to celebrate the opening of the Panama Canal. The city had put up many new buildings to impress visitors.

Tom Hanks was a scientist with the U.S. Geological Survey. He explained: "Engineers used 1906 rubble to fill in the shallow water of the Marina District for exposition buildings. They pumped in mud and sand and didn't properly compact it."[4] Later, homes and other buildings were placed on this unstable soil. During the 1989 quake, the shaking stirred up this soil. It became mixed up with groundwater, which turned into a liquid substance. The buildings then sank into this mush.

Thousands of people in the Marina district and other stricken areas were suddenly homeless. Tent cities and other shelters sprang up to fill the need. The Marina Middle School was among the places where victims could find shelter and other help. Red Cross workers placed chairs and cots in the gymnasium. They provided meals and clothing for the victims.

Gretchen Wells, her husband, and their one-year-old son had just moved into their condominium less than three months earlier. The final painting and work inside were just finished the day of the quake. "There's damage everywhere. Virtually every wall and ceiling in this place is going to have to come down in terms of the plaster and the molding, and the exterior type things," Wells said.[5]

Many victims in the San Francisco Bay Area faced

worse problems than just fixing up their homes. The city of Oakland already had a serious problem with homelessness. Now more than twenty-five hundred people were added to the list of those without homes. Betty Pitts and her children were among these new homeless people. Pitts was frustrated when she and her children could not find a place to stay. Said Pitts, "Everybody says there's a

A bulldozer brings down a damaged apartment building in the Marina District of San Francisco as people watch from the roof of another building.

*F*irefighters search through the rubble of crumbling homes. Many people were left homeless, following the earthquake's devastating effects.

list for this and a list for that. What kind of emergency aid is that? I need a safe place now, not next week."[6]

In the wake of the disaster, many people tried to keep a positive attitude. The Peterson family was among them. They showed journalist Thomas Canby their ruined home in the Loma Prieta area. Mrs. Peterson said, "It's just a house. We still have our lives, our pictures—I still have my wedding dress." She warned Canby of ongoing danger: "This place is still settling. If you hear a creaking, go for a door."[7]

As they worked to help themselves, quake victims were also impressed with the help they received from

This large get-well card for six-year-old Julio Berumen is just one of many he received from people all over the country. Others are stacked around it.

others. Immediately following the quake, hundreds of volunteers came forward to aid the injured.

At shelters volunteers carried supplies, cooked and served food, read to frightened children, and consoled the elderly. Outdoors they helped homeowners look for lost pets, clear debris, and make repairs. People offered their spare rooms to families whose homes had been destroyed. Volunteers gave rides to people who had lost their cars in the quake. Residents with flashlights helped to direct traffic on streets where signal lights were no longer working. Restaurants served free meals on the streets. Some hotels opened their doors to people who had no home to go to, and could not afford to pay for a room.

People from around the country sent donations to aid victims. Six-year-old Julio Berumen received many get-well cards and toys. The children's hospital received donations of money for Julio and other children who had suffered from the quake.

Sherra Cox was injured and lost her home and possessions. She expressed gratitude for the help she received. "I learned how kind and wonderful people are. You don't realize how many friends you have until something like this happens," said Cox.[8]

This outpouring of concern was a bright spot during a grim time. Dr. James Betts was part of a rescue crew. He said, "There were hundreds of individuals, thousands perhaps, . . . people just off the street participated in doing miraculous things. I think the whole community came together very quickly."[9]

CHAPTER 4

Day-to-Day Struggles

The quake itself caused plenty of damage. But that was only the beginning. When buildings are moved around and shattered, gas pipes and electrical lines break. These broken lines caused numerous fires that spread through San Francisco, Oakland, and Berkeley.

The World Series was postponed for ten days. Oakland manager Tony La Russa said, "If the A's are going to be celebrating, the celebration isn't going to be the same."[1]

Sixty-three people had died as a result of the San Francisco Bay Area earthquake. Four people died during the destruction that occurred in Santa Cruz. Another person died when the Bay Bridge caved in. Several others lost their lives inside a building in San Francisco. About thirty-eight hundred others were injured.

Federal officials declared seven counties in northern California as disaster areas. City building inspectors worked overtime checking damaged buildings. They had to decide whether buildings were safe or unsafe. Buildings

The American flag is flown at half-staff in honor of earthquake victims, as Game 3 of the 1989 World Series is resumed at Oakland Coliseum.

were inspected and assigned a color-coded ticket. A green tag meant the residents could move back in. Unsafe buildings received red tags, meaning they could not be occupied. Many families found themselves "red-tagged."

One family waited anxiously while an inspector examined their home. Gloria Cary, age sixty-one, had lived in the Marina District for years with her daughter and three children. When the inspector was done, he said, "I think it's salvageable."[2] More than one hundred thousand homes and businesses were damaged.

For weeks to come, people suffered from the ongoing effects of the quake. Many activities of day-to-day life were inconvenient at best. In the beginning, water, electricity, and gas services were interrupted. Telephones also did not work normally.

Many people had problems with transportation. Five freeways were shut down. The San Francisco International Airport was also closed for several weeks.

People in many walks of life lost income after the quake. Tourism to the area declined greatly. People canceled vacations to the San Francisco Bay Area for months after the earthquake. Said cab driver Breck Alexander, people had left San Francisco "in droves."[3]

Pastor Berumen, the father of miracle survivor Julio, was among the many people who lost time at work. His wife had died in her car during the quake. Berumen stayed home for several months caring for Julio and his sister, Cathy. Julio worked hard to learn to walk with his artificial leg and a brace. Berumen said, "I want the children to lead a normal life."[4]

Economic losses were estimated at $6 billion. Bay Area residents asked for money to rebuild businesses and homes. They filed applications totaling $550 million with FEMA—the Federal Emergency Management Administration.

Homelessness remained a big problem. By the end of November, some 240 buildings were still judged unsafe.

A parking lot turns into a campground for many people who were displaced by the earthquake. The quake forced the evacuation of many people from their homes.

Hundreds of people remained in city shelters. Thousands of others were living in temporary housing.

As Thanksgiving approached, Katherine Simpson and her two children were still homeless. They had a small, fixed income. Before the quake they lived in a rent-controlled apartment. Afterward, Simpson, a nurse and single mother, had to move her family into a motel. The situation was especially difficult because three-year-old Sam had serious health problems. He was wheelchair-bound.

Each day Simpson spent hours searching for another apartment. She became frustrated when numerous Red Cross workers could not find the family a place to live. Simpson became more and more worried about Sam. He needed a great deal of care and had become withdrawn after the earthquake. The dust in the air at the motel was making him sicker. Finally, just before Thanksgiving, the Simpsons were able to move into another apartment.

For others, especially commuters, transportation remained the worst problem. In late November the Bay Bridge reopened. However, some of the ramps remained closed. The Embarcadero Highway and some other highways were not yet back in business. Structural engineers doubted if they could be fixed at all.

The Cypress Freeway that had crossed West Oakland was completely destroyed. As a result, a twelve-mile trip now took one hour. Before the quake, more than fifty thousand cars used this freeway each day. After the quake, they had to use a two-lane connector to the Bay Bridge.

Quake victims sought support from friends and

*P*assengers ride the ferry from Oakland to San Francisco. When the Bay Bridge was damaged, ferry service between the two cities was provided for commuters.

relatives. Psychologists reported that thousands of quake victims were suffering from anxiety, fear, depression, or other emotional problems.

Political leaders offered words of encouragement. Art Agnos, the mayor of San Francisco, expressed optimism a month after the quake. He praised citizens for their courage and hard work. Mayor Agnos also pushed the federal government to quickly send the aid it had promised. Agnos said, "I want to make . . .sure we have the kind of commitments and follow-through that takes care of the people that have suffered in our city."[5]

CHAPTER 5

The Long Road to Recovery

As weeks passed, life was still far from normal. Thousands of people were still living in tent shelters and other temporary housing. People who had lost their cars could not drive to work or to school. Those whose homes had been destroyed were living out of suitcases. They lacked clothing and basic household items that they needed.

Some people were still missing and were feared dead in the wreckage from the quake. People begged search crews to look for missing friends and relatives. The police arrested some people who disobeyed official orders not to search for missing people on their own. Friends of Robin Ortiz said they planned to look for her after search crews gave up. Ortiz had worked at a coffeehouse located in the Pacific Garden Mall. The mall was destroyed by the quake. "I know she's in there," said family friend Betty Barnes.[1] When crews finally did return to the scene, they found Ortiz's body in the wreckage.

Several schools were demolished or so badly damaged that they were closed after the quake. For hundreds of young people, classes were interrupted for weeks.

The shortage of low-income housing was another serious problem. This type of housing was older and more run-down than the city's more expensive housing. The quake had destroyed about fifteen hundred units in residential hotels in downtown San Francisco.

Rescue crews and search dogs, in front of a destroyed house in the Marina District of San Francisco, continue to search for any possible victims.

Before October 17 the city was already short of low-income housing. Now the situation became critical. Mayor Agnos and other city officials asked federal officials for help. "What we're asking them for is to give us the money we need to rebuild those units."[2]

The earthquake also destroyed abandoned buildings where homeless people had been living. These homeless people were now even worse off than they were before the quake. Many of them were still living in trailers a year after the quake.

Many people helped their neighbors after the quake, but some dishonest people took advantage of the disaster. A few stores charged extra-high prices for flashlights, water, and other things that people needed to survive. Theives posed as building inspectors in order to enter homes they wanted to rob.

In late November television crews visited the famous Fisherman's Wharf area. They found empty streets. Jay Horner, a hotel manager at the wharf, spoke to reporters. He pointed to the streets and empty parking spots in near-by lots. He said, "Generally, the streets are packed with tourists. You'll see many, many joggers up and down the Fisherman's Wharf area, parking lots are [usually] over-flowing. . . ."[3]

Owners of museums and shops also said that business was slow. Some places were closing early at night. Stores in the popular Union Square area did not have as many customers as usual. One shoe store manager said, "They're not coming to the city. They're afraid."[4]

A stuffed bear and photo albums were left behind as a family rushed to removed valuables from their home, following the earthquake. Residents were given only fifteen minutes to remove things they could carry.

One year after the quake, signs of the disaster still lingered. Some stores were still boarded up. A number of houses remained off their foundations. People who had been displaced were still sleeping in trailers or on the streets. There was still not enough low-income housing. Many of the people who had lost jobs and businesses as a result of quake damage were now working at lower-paying jobs.

Preparations had been made in case another quake struck. San Francisco increased its fire-fighting forces. The city added more trucks, ambulances, and fireboats. More people joined neighborhood fire corps.

An organization called Dignity Housing West offered its help. This group of private and government organizations led efforts to restore buildings that could house needy people. Terry Messman worked with Dignity Housing West. He said, "Three years after the earthquake, most earthquake victims are still having a very hard time finding replacement housing."[5]

Commuters continued to adjust to the results of the quake. It took almost eight years before the Cypress Freeway in Oakland was completely rebuilt. Residents of West Oakland had disliked the location of the old highway. They pressured officials to move the new highway farther west. The new roadway skirted the San Francisco Bay.

On July 23, 1997, the expressway reopened. Commuters could once again use this five-mile stretch to travel between San Francisco and Oakland. For thousands of people, a commuting nightmare had ended at last.

Drivers make their way through a damaged, cracked roadway, following the devastating earthquake.

The new rebuilt highway was made strong enough to withstand a quake measuring 7.5 on the Richter scale. It cost $1 billion. News anchorman Brian Williams said, "It's now mile for mile the most expensive stretch of highway in the United States."[6]

Will people be more prepared the next time a big earthquake strikes? Scientists around the world have worked to find more reliable ways to predict these disasters. One possible sign of approaching quakes are foreshocks—weak tremors that may come before larger quakes. Scientists are also seeking ways to measure the amount of stress in the earth's crust. They want to find

*T*raffic moves smoothly along the Golden Gate Bridge into the city of San Francisco, following the earthquake.

out how the earth's magnetic field changes before a quake. They wonder if the land surface tilts or bulges in ways that can be observed. Some scientists are exploring the possibility that animals can sense an oncoming quake. If so, their behavior may change just before a quake occurs.

Would the ability to predict earthquakes be truly useful? Some people think not. They worry what would happen if an earthquake were predicted for a heavily populated city. Millions of frightened people might try to leave all at once. This would create chaos. People would probably also not be able to flee in time.

Since, for now, quakes cannot be predicted with great accuracy, efforts are made to prevent and minimize the damage they cause. Some people believe that nothing should be built on or near a known fault. This has not happened, however. People continue to build homes and other buildings in earthquake-prone areas.

Buildings can be put together in ways that make them more "earthquake-resistant." Steel is used to reinforce tall buildings. Buildings can also be made so that they bend slightly instead of collapsing during a quake. Architects have designed simpler structures without heavy ornaments that could break off. House foundations are constructed with extra concrete that will keep them in place if the earth vibrates.

Some buildings have systems that can lessen the vibrations earthquakes cause. Special motion sensors show when the building starts to move. A computer system then takes over. It figures out how much weight must be moved to offset that force. The computer signals a movable weight on top of the building. It shifts the appropriate amount of weight into the right position.

What about changes in elevated highways? The collapse of the Nimitz Freeway caused most of the deaths in the San Francisco Bay Area earthquake. Engineers are studying ways to support elevated roadways so that their columns stay in place.

Fire prevention is a major goal. Gas pipes and electrical lines can be built with flexible joints. Working water

*R*escue workers continue their search for survivors, following the earthquake. The area marked with a red circle shows a spot where a survivor is believed to be.

lines are essential if fires do break out. Water lines can be made so they stay intact during a quake.

Inside their homes people can also take precautions. They can keep heavy objects away from high shelves. They can bolt shelving units and bookcases securely to wooden supports inside the walls of a room. Closet doors must also be secured so that the contents do not spill out and cause injuries during a quake.

Long after an earthquake, people still feel its effects. A school psychologist in California said that children in her school are on the alert for new earthquakes. She says, "If something shakes, they'll just look at me with these big eyes and say, 'Is this it again?' They're very serious when we have an earthquake drill. There's no fooling around."[7]

Mayor Art Agnos agrees: "No one has forgotten the earthquake—and no one will ever forget it."[8]

Writing for the *San Francisco Chronicle*, Randy Shilts had this to say:

> I think we all believe that we are the masters of the universe. We, in our enlightened age, have clean water, and we have heat, and we have all these things that we never question. And then something like this happens, and you realize that we are small creatures still.[9]

Other Major Earthquakes in United States History

YEAR	CITY	RICHTER MAGNITUDE
April 1906	San Francisco, California	7.9
March 27, 1964	Anchorage, Alaska	9.2
February 9, 1971	Los Angeles, California	6.5
October 17, 1989	San Francisco–Oakland, California	7.1
January 18, 1994	Los Angeles, California	7.1

Chapter 1. Fifteen Seconds of Destruction

1. Ed Magnuson, "Earthquake!" *Time*, October 30, 1989, p. 34.
2. Tom Callahan, "Baseball Calls Time," *Newsweek*, October 30, 1989, p. 48.
3. Thomas Y. Canby, "Earthquake: Prelude to the Big One?" *National Geographic*, May 1990, p. 87.
4. Magnuson, p. 34.
5. NBC Television, *Today*, November 21, 1989.
6. Ibid.

Chapter 2. Rumblings of Disaster

1. Thomas Y. Canby, "Earthquake: Prelude to the Big One," *National Geographic*, May 1990, p. 89.

Chapter 3. Miracle Survivors

1. Thomas Y. Canby, "Earthquake: Prelude to the Big One?" *National Geographic*, May 1990, p. 79.
2. Ed Magnuson, "Earthquake!" *Time*, October 30, 1989, pp. 30–31.
3. "Picking Up the Pieces," *People*, October 22, 1990, p. 34.
4. Canby, p. 90.
5. NBC Television, *Today*, November 21, 1989, from Burrelle's transcripts, p. 1.
6. Eloise Salholz et al., "Recovery by the Bay," *Newsweek*, November 6, 1989, p. 40.
7. Canby, p. 91.
8. "Picking Up the Pieces," *People*, October 22, 1990, p. 34.
9. NBC Television, *Today*, November 21, 1989.

Chapter 4. Day-to-Day Struggles

1. Tom Callahan, "Baseball Calls Time," *Newsweek*, October 30, 1989, p. 48.

2. Thomas Y. Canby, "Earthquake: Prelude to the Big One," *National Geographic*, May 1990, p. 90.

3. NBC Television, *Today*, November 21, 1989, from Burrelle's transcripts, p. 25.

4. "Picking Up the Pieces," *People*, October 22, 1990, p. 34.

5. Eloise Salholz et al., "Recovery by the Bay," *Newsweek*, November 6, 1989, p. 37.

Chapter 5. The Long Road to Recovery

1. Ed Magnuson, "Earthquake!" *Time*, October 30, 1989, p. 39.

2. NBC Television, *Today*, November 21, 1989.

3. Ibid.

4. Ibid.

5. *NBC News at Sunrise*, May 29, 1997.

6. MSNBC, *The News*, July 23, 1997, from Burrelle's transcripts, p. 8.

7. David Gelman, "Coping With Quake Fear," *Newsweek*, October 30, 1989, p. 47.

8. "Picking Up the Pieces," *People*, October 22, 1990, p. 33.

9. Quoted in The Tide Foundation, *Fifteen Seconds: The Great California Earthquake of 1989* (Covelo, Calif.: Island Press, 1989), frontispiece.

aftershock—Vibrations in the earth that come after an earthquake.

epicenter—The area where damage is likely to be most severe during an earthquake.

fault—A place where rocks beneath the earth's surface have cracked and pulled away from their normal positions.

Federal Emergency Management Administration (FEMA)—An agency run by the federal government. It helps victims of disasters.

geologist—A scientist who studies the history and structure of the earth.

normal fault—A place beneath the earth's surface where one side of two opposite pieces of rock has been pulled downward.

plate—A large piece of rock in the earth's crust.

reverse fault—A place beneath the earth's surface where two sides of rock are shoved together, causing one side to move higher than the other one.

Richter scale—A standard system for measuring the strength of an earthquake.

seismic waves—Waves of energy that spread from the original site of an earthquake.

seismograph—A device that shows earthquake waves.

seismologist—A scientist who studies earthquakes.

strike-slip fault—A type of fault that runs up and down. In this type of fault, one piece of the earth's outer rocky shell has moved past the rock on the opposite side.

Books

Archer, Jules. *Earthquake!* Parsippany, N.J.: Crestwood House, 1991.

Booth, Basil. *Volcanoes and Earthquakes.* Parsippany, N.J.: New Discovery Books, 1990.

Cleary, Margot Keam. *Great Disasters of the Twentieth Century.* New York: Gallery Books, 1990.

Cleeve, Roger. *The Earth.* Englewood Cliffs, N.J.: Prentice Hall, 1990.

Davis, Lee. *Natural Disasters.* New York: Facts on File, 1992.

Haddock, Patricia. *San Francisco.* Parsippany, N.J.: Dillon Press, 1989.

Keller, David. *Great Disasters: The Most Shocking Moments in History.* New York: Avon, 1990.

Lampton, Christopher. *Earthquake.* Brookfield, Conn.: The Millbrook Press, 1994.

Mariner, Tom, and Anyon Ellis. *Book of the Earth.* Parsippany, N.J.: Dillon Press, 1995.

Spies, Karen Bornemann. *Earthquakes.* New York: Twenty-First Century Books, 1994.

Internet Sites

Loma Prieta Earthquake
<http://www.eqe.com/publications/lomaprie/ lomaprie.htm>

Quake of '89
<http://www.kron.com/specials/89quake/main.html>